The Passage Of Time

poetry **Pt** *today*

THE PASSAGE OF TIME

Edited by
Rebecca Mee

First published in Great Britain in 1998 by Poetry
Today, an imprint of
Penhaligon Page Ltd, 12 Godric Square, Maxwell Road,
Peterborough. PE2 7JJ

A Catalogue record for this book is available from the
British Library

ISBN 1 86226 510 0

Typesetting and layout, Penhaligon Page Ltd, England.
Printed and bound by Forward Press Ltd, England

Foreword

The Passage Of Time is a compilation of poetry, featuring some of our finest poets. The book gives an insight into the essence of modern living and deals with the reality of life today. We think we have created an anthology with a universal appeal.

There are many technical aspects to the writing of poetry and *The Passage Of Time* contains free verse and examples of more structured work from a wealth of talented poets.

Poetry is a coat of many colours. Today's poets write in a limitless array of styles: traditional rhyming poetry is as alive and kicking today as modern free-verse. Language ranges from easily accessible to intricate and elusive.

Poems have a lot to offer in our fast-paced 'instant' world. Reading poems gives us an opportunity to sit back and explore ourselves and the world around us.

Contents

Flies

Flies enact the innocent drama

in the grass

they spar

fall

and spar again;

I adopt the critics deluded role.

Chris North

Nell

Endless tape and steamless time what mistresses are they,
Yet so they are rated.
In time and breadth so many numbers are recorded
For inspection.
From Blackhall Street down whence I slid
Those gentlemen upon the Clyde the torch have passed
As in a relay, far too long, the baton,
Here a log with names inscribed and little more.
My secret history thus confined
Is locked beyond my hold.

The measure now of what I say is as quicksilver
Gone before the thought is formed.
Something of fear a little mixed with joy. A boy, maybe?
An ancient man... who knows has trod these boards
In all these years
Off Malin and in Hebrides.
Lost memories of ocean lie astern as drives streams of salt
Shed from the carapace of my soul.
Future's history where I'm bound; lay off my course
And let me run.

Trail vortices unite and gurgle on your way,
Cut forward with my chain and tear asunder
That which is writ today.
Take harbour in my sensuality,
My ample hips of oak.
Dance once again upon my deck, as you have done before
(with strict awareness of my age).
Skip, Howl and scream as you are able
Without a thought of time,
For *this* is my dimension.

David Frowde Stabb

Dutch Elm

The stump - cleanly severed
yearly circles open
to the sky;
each one a line -
upon a human face,
the agony of age
exposed;
the bark a mask -
world weary, flaking off,
fungus in its place - and
beneath, an insect
world -
within a world
gnawing at decay.

Peter Cranswick

Missing

There is no grave on which to lay a flower;
there is no rite I know to mark your passing.
All is improvised of pain.
My memory of you leaves so little
a tiny textbook figure on a screen:
sunk in your dark sea;
and a feeling I once carried.

Rosalind Hughes

The Masters Of Surprise
(An industrial comedy in four cantos)

....So....say goodbye to all this and bide your uneasy time,
this living 'Camera Obscura' moves its all seeing eye a little
further down the aisle.
Soon the Wedding Feast will haste to heal this petty rift,
this ship of stranded souls, keel-hauled and set adrift.
Onward, into Civilisation's beckoning furrow,
though bondaged now, we'll all be free tomorrow!
Scarce solace my friend, for these, their cry unheeded,
a shallow future waits only upon some scanty European...........
Death to this *Latex Strangler,* this ripper of mosaic souls,
I'll write him obscene fan letters, and send him all my love!
But you: you grip the armchair and worship at the rail;
Hours Of Mindless Drivel is the bread and wine of your faith,
'Quiz' and 'Chat' are the holy relics of this worthless creed;
smiling, catatonic faces nailed to the symbols of their greed
serenade you with sermons of how good their lives have been,
and there you sit, and share some portion of their excess
while all around you your insignificant life collapses.
Vetted, positive that the game was fairly played,
and no favours dubiously bought for heavy subscriptions paid.
You Angelic Sot! Blinded by the light of their sheer honesty
your smile, vacant-like, misses the whole point of its sheer
tenacity.........
oh...... rant on, my friend, you'll never change that much,
and all your vicious ravings will surely vanish into dust.
The twilight protracts another day of indecent exposures,
of failed promises and blithe, indifferent confessions.
Night descends and refutes these smothered graves;
The Masters Of Surprise, Kings of all that they survey
turn the page,
and all their faults and favours drift silently.......... away...

Christopher Hayes

Requiem

Soundless as the tenebrous twilight, we gathered round
that dank December day; when mists hugged the ground.
And autumn, quietly mourned, sank slowly beneath the winter
streets,
Solemn, flanked with burnished-copper leaves of head hung

beech.

The children came to together. Hers, ours, those of others,
lives she had touched upon though being a mother.

Within the firelight, in sibling conversations,
speaking hesitantly of her, with, at first, doubted elation.
Each with an urge to recall her in words, upon the cusp of which
a tear would gently stir, teeter soft but brief, before being warmed
by a smile, and the fond memories we recounted more than once

in a while.

Their heartfelt words offered comfort and prompted mutual

reminiscence,
but perhaps saw not her withered limbs or felt the lingering chill

of Death's
late presence. But each spoken memory gave substance to the

litany of her life
and its recent end, without which she could not, her wearying pain,

transcend.

The falling flames suggested our finiteness, in the embers I

sensed a heart beat
fade, falter, then finally cease, the dying warmth a symbol of how
her selfless life did finally, ease.

The quiet sealing of her lips, as soundless as a snowflake's fall,
ere the whispered whiteness of sleep enfolded, released her and
became her pall.

So fitting she should leave us when our thoughts, childlike, run to
past years. Christmases at her side, so distant, but ever clear.

6

Her life, although a memory, was a once-fierce flame that has faded,
yet has other flames fulfilled, which now blaze unaided.
That given spark shines far beyond our momentary mourning
                                    and the
gaping absence of her light, from where the many memories of her,
though fleeting, ever burn bright . . .

Dennis Martin

This Century:

A Hindenburg concerto of hydrogen booms. The wombs of
Hiroshima, washing
out death. The Kennedy head is gone--and on, and on, and on. I
want to erase such devastation. The damage is irreparable. All I can
do is to sympathise with those seeing signs of severed ties: the black-
eye witnesses of witlessness who talk to my heart through each article
of burning-Buddhist footage. May Fortune side with the resilient.

Russell Moxham

The Hero

Joseph led geese
blind to waterfront.
Surge said the front
drag pebbles 'neath
His geese feet,
when out they
set calling 'round
the chillthin waist
an' blue rib hands,
to crackle
the Hero's
last call for theirs
drowned 'neath the
crowding surge.

Matt Hill

Season's End

The roundabout circles more slowly
To disjointed janglings
Suspended on wrought iron and oil;
The last coconut falls on canvas
And rolls to rest
With quiet sawdust on its hairs.

Snarling truth
Gnaws though the toffee
To the seedy core,
To the fingers of the future
Faded pink against grey autumn sands.

Barbara Harvey Jones

Flux

(*Imperious caesar, dead and turn'd to clay
Might stop a hole to keep the wind away.*)
Hamlet.

The mummy drawn this day from out a weeping bog
is of today, no less today's that any infant born today;
no more of yesterday than this day's dawn.
The alteration of the thing they placed among the reeds
ten thousand years ago;
each chemic change by which each day's wan thing
became some other thing,
other than that which lay there through the day before,
matched those swift cell divisions, tissue formulations,
egg to embryo, that had made each babe.

No sword-thrust of some vengeful past
can make us bleed.
No shout of horror from the field of Agincourt,
nor other such sad sound of other time
can hurt us now,
nor could a peal of laughter from the Globe
bring cheer to present ear.
Of those events, and of their people
we can know
what we have read, by others writ,
what we have heard, by other tongues bespoke,
all of it only otherness.
The monuments and the sculptures
songs and art and other works,
seen now by this day's eyes
and heard by this day's ears.

Time past, time present
time present, time future
all time past is now past,
time future we cannot know,
only in time present is reality.

We have no need to argue nor need we seek to prove
that some event of some brief moment of the past.
Not only had its that-time truth
but in some part was cause of that which followed after.
Connections there were, but what they were
we cannot know beyond question,
we cannot test, we cannot prove,
and, present logic that persuades us now
may later prove most sadly weak.

G L Kesteven

Berzerkers

Cages locked full of thirsty men watching
Rivers afloat with the guilt edge flowers of doom
All souls raised to the power of One
Once heard in battle but lost on the shimmering winds.

Fill up the cages, release the vats
Watch the throb of ultra-violent rage;
Encompassed, enthralled, eternal love lost on the ground
Wishes drift on a wing and a prayer
Everything is still, everything is now.

The call comes and fetid fields fill the air
Ferocious savages dined on the witches' potent brew
Down levers and escape to the future
Hearts on their cuffs served up to the monsters' din.

Hellfire burning in their eyes
Fear falling foul of the brew.
No transcendence in the hazy glow of flight
A cacophony of woe bursts through the flames.

The Berzerkers are realised, the battle is drawn
Warriors eaten up on the field, hyperreal ships
Waiting for their spoils.
Dispatching to death for the love: Valhalla
Living up to the call.

Berzerkers rule the world that's all.

Aileann Reel

The Song The Sirens Sang

Before the Celts to Ireland came
Or Stonehenge mapped the sun,
A sailor sailed the wine-dark sea
And so this riddle spun.

His crew, they bound him to the mast
(With wax he'd stopped their ears),
For none must hear the demon song,
Said he, to calm their fears.

On naked rocks the sirens lay,
Their lissom limbs lapped in the foam,
With wild hair streaming in the wind
That bore their voices' burthen, Come!

While rowers toiled upon their oars
Oblivious to the lotus pang,
He heard, in his dread odyssey,
The song the sirens sang.

He strove in vain against his bonds
As taunting, haunting came their plea:
Come, rest upon these silken sands -
You will forget Penelope.

His senses swam in looks of love,
In pain and ecstasy he broke
All vows - thus passed the enchanted isle
Whose lustful incense palled like smoke . . .

Ere Arab keels sought China's shores
Or Egypt bowed to Rome,
A sailor sailed the wine-dark sea,
His thoughts turned towards home.

In Ithaca he brooded long
Nor joyed again in the salt-sea tang,
And none there were dared ask of him
What song the sirens sang.

D Goodbrand

Born To Sleep

Face down,
  Into the softness
Of curled feathers,
  Eyes closed,
Dreams
  Behind the human curtains,
The eyelids,
  To hide behind reality,
Curled up,
  In a womb like position,
With no disturbance,
  Enclosed by the warmth
Of the feather down,
  The haven of sleep.

Della Clark

The Whisperer

Walls seldom whisper
at least if this were
true, I would cease to
wonder who or what
to do. In case the
cracks would grow
and creep on tip toe,
the silence would be
broken as the walls
no more. The wall
is my barrier against
time and natures will,
though the pressure it
withstands really makes
the thrill. How long
before its shell like
pattern is destroyed,
its structure now
without meaning,
its crumbling releases
me from the torment,
so reuniting me will make
me stand once more.

Munir A Yoozooph

Epitaph On A Defunct Clock

And now time ceases to exist.
If a clock stops, battery exhausted,
We know that it's no longer 10 o'clock
At night or in the morning.
That was yesterday's time
Which will start again
On reconnection.

But now we have timelessness
In perpetuity.

Robert Hewett

Taking Out A Mortgage On Vesuvius

'Why don't ya
Take out a mortgage, huh?
Take out a mortgage on Vesuvius, hey!
Boy is that a neat hill.'

The mannequin rides darkly by
Along the pillow line,
Its simian head and pointed ears
Obsidian, malign.

'Skip a dee do dah,
Skip a dee day!
Have us a ball, wow,
An auto da fe!'

The voices erupts like debris
From a live volcanic deep,
Whence living masquerades of hell
Disturb the eye of sleep.

Graham Meadows

Expert

Hard? I do it standing on my head. No pills.
More often sitting. No blocks. No fancy mechanisms.
Or sprawling, variously angled, over pillows.
Three nights a week, specially three days a month
Mere flesh wide opens, one of my shrinking number target
For the sweet spill of your millions.
Fire? You keep firing, darling.
I needn't move a muscle to kill them.

Georgina Lock

Sunday Badgers

Responding, as guests should, to eager invitation,
though comfortable with friends and wine,
I scuttled after the rest
into the darkness of the styled suburban garden,
beat through swirling mists of nipping midge,
negotiated rockery shelves
slippery with summer rain,
to a gap in the hedge.
There,
conspirators all, hushed and hopeful,
subtly hissing for silence,
we waited as the laden evening clung and hummed . . .
Only a moment.
I saw just the one, perhaps young (what do I know?)
as it stood with a brief, blind stare,
toddled a bit,
cuter than Disney,
then disappeared beyond my precarious, huddled focus
to continue the business of frolicking
elsewhere.
I thought it happy,
but not as happy as I was
to be there.

Sue Duffield

October Requiem
For M O Suttaby, Muskoka, Canada

Is this the fifth or sixth time I've made this trip?
Dear God, I'm tired
- even before the car arrives
where an old woman huddles in bed
like a drift of leaves beneath an early snow.

Death I can handle (just).
it's the dusty withering that gets me down.
Thank God for the trees, anyway,
crackling redly past beside the road
beneath an ageing sky
as the years leaves die joyfully.

They've got the technique, those maples
- after how many million years of practice?
Threescore and ten just isn't enough . . .
Yet what if we began at birth?
Enough sparks might be struck
to ignite our last days.

We are a deciduous race.
Before the frost we should bask and blaze,
each bright leaf a banner
hailing beds made
invalids fed
pain ignored
a little laughter . . .
Being human, and therefore proud, stubborn and sad,
we specialise in leaves withered and brown.
Yet the eternal earth sends us out with peels of scarlet glory
into the long sleep
- and then, when we had given up waiting,
water running under snow,
and trumpets in the sky.

Mary Sylvia Winter

Looking Down Into A Valley At Dawn

Walking in mist and early dew,
grass squeaking softly undershoes
flicking bare ankles
and standing hairs on end.

Good God! Give me a swift heart attack,
the last whip's crack:
My head spirals to the side
and comes to rest on a sod.

Flirty little birds come nearer and nearer -
go to sleep in the damp and
they'll peck your eyes out.
A musty smell, and, all of a sudden
your locking knees can't carry you away
from the shores of the Lake of Fire.

Kevin Walbank

Zlodski's Thought Transference

I see:
Winged horses and unicorns,
Flying and galloping on meadows of green,
An orange sky with a complementary blue sun,
Is this, the land of tomorrow?
Or the land of never been?
The stallion on the wing is strong and bold,
His mare beside him is his guide and inspiration,
And the rainbow is full,
And so is the pot of gold,
By a lemonade lake two elves are fishing,
A boy and a girl with red hats and blue shoes too,
And each with a matching silver bell,
For they intend to land the great pink salmon,
For that they are now wishing.

Jonathan Simms

Did You Ever Think?

Cadavers and corpses rotting in yards
Tombstones of actors, poets and bards
These are the things you see when you stroll
Through trees and shrubs surrounding these holes

'Coz they're all now the same when stuck in the earth
No fame, no humour and definitely no mirth
But what if they could sit up and see themselves now?
Look in the mirror at their dead weathered brow

Would they all stand aloof as they did so in life?
Or go back and visit the trouble and strife?
'How's it going darling? Sorry I'm late!
Haunt the neighbours children into terrible states?

God what a giggle, I bet they are smirking
Scaring and spooking with the chains and the lurking
Moving statues and curtains when you're home all alone
Scraping and scratching and such terrible moans

Drive you mad to distraction until you finally do drop
Clutching your heart as it draws to a stop
Or do they just lay in their coffins so terribly dead?
No reincarnation tunnels despite what is said

Definitely gone when the candles snuffed out
And dead means dead, of that there's no doubt
What a terrible thought that is for those left here and lonely
Remembering their loved ones in photo memories only

So I prefer to remember them sneaking back to play
Riding in on the breeze at the end of the day
Having a laugh in their lives in the world from beyond
Checking up on loved ones they remember so fond

They're not all the same in my mind whatever you may think
They're here all around us kicking up a stink
One's standing beside me maybe and editing this work
I know that 'coz my pen's gone missing again and it's driving me
berserk!

Mark Ford

Things To Do Today

Dear Manchunian
You have travelled far
I paved these streets with gold, you see
Especially for you to come to me.

Oh love.
Not much in south-east London
Across New Cross
Blackheath and Plumstead common.

Small price to pay you see
A radio and a cup of tea
I find it hard to believe that God is watching me

Can't smile about my future
Can't lie about my past
Something's slowly creeping in-between me and the people
                                        I once loved.

Here's a tale to tell
Here's a soul who fell
This is why I'm here you see
Especially for you to talk to me

Oh love,
Not much in south-east London
Across New Cross
Bring your heart through Blackwall Tunnel,
                            come on!

Pippa Beavis

Dog-Escape . . .

Snarl of wolf on steppes, what hungry packs
Fought and tore within this golden shape
Became the gentle thing now tamely leased?
And yet a lien remains: marvel of nose
That start-up swiftness straight from sleep . . . look
At helter-skelter run across the flatland
Taking plough and yard-wide water ditches
With eager stride and bugle-tongue, closing
On jinking hare, or stag-like, paws together
Leaping in tall grass, porpoise-appearing,
Or disdaining steps upon a stile
Sweet-leaping over in parabola . . .
Ranging the country far day-long untiring.

Sudden escaping nimble-featly
Into the wind of early morning
Finds every corner here and there,
Cock-legged, curious, nose-aware,
Nose seeking, finding, knowing
The maddening scent of running hare,
Exploding then, legs jack-knifing
Into furious gallop, chasing
That tiny kangaroo-legged thing
In crazy pace through fields beyond,
Far into the moors and hills,
Away, away . . . wonderfully gone . . .

Then worthy of that feral dog pack
Of fighting, delighting, wandering things,
Jostling, chasing on the steppes
With onager and tarpan horse
Far from ragged little men?
Blasphemy then
To hear untuneful master voice
Threatening to beat and raving
About some wicked dog! . . . submitting
To angry shackle, prison house
Like any slave . . .

Austin Cooper

Glimpse

To abscond momentarily did
the world evaporate so
fell through a sifting fog of
warmed opaque chances where
grey spectral sculptures remained grazing
peacefully as ever hidden
on that other side
Derelict
to those assumptions once so admired
And
time adorned in white carnations chased
the fuchsias blood red smiles down to that tide where
such salty glitz voluminous azure gnashed a
punitive chorus at that infernal sun under which
those silent myopic creatures traced
the treacherous coral so
sliced all conscience and
were gone.

Simon J Veal

Tears No Longer Flow

Pills or pethidine modify
Response from our souls.
Beta-blockers bridle emotions,
Once wild stallions inhaling incense
From friendly grass around hooves,
Horseshoed from the fervent earth.

Mother, why do tears
Never streak your face?
When moisture threatens
Fragile flesh on all sides of eyes,
Drops stagger, stutter out over the
Shattered shroud of a dated accessory.

Feelings forced out, child
Only through shocked doses
Of heroin, cocaine; momentary contact
With a deeper intuition . . . slipping into oblivion.

I do not feel these lines jotted down
From so deep a void unveiled.

Wait, tears babble out;
I am free, I am me!

Michele Glazer

Tempus

The night man calls in silence
Watching, waiting
Greyly smiling at God's joke
The hour of three all's well
Yet little time to pray
Before the dawn
But who needs prayer?

There is always a call
Remembrance
Of some far distant scene
When dawn and time and prayer
Were one, praising the Universe

The night man calls
Voice absolving, whispering
Late, but not too late for whispering
Hushed prayer, ashamedly forgetful
Forgetfulness and prayer are synonymous
I listen and I listen.

Alex Macdonald

Sight Restored

Pot-plants set on slow-drip mat,
windows closed, alarms set,
housekey with neighbours,
milk order on hold -
the day of escape has come.

Mind racing, anticipating
moonscape of rocks, alpine stars
shining up from limestone grikes,
within sight of Atlantic rolling, curling,
soothing sand and rattling shells.

The shout of the wind dies to a whisper:
silence, stillness, the busy world stops.

Idly mooching round village shops,
lulled by the potter's whirring wheel,
bemused by clunk clunk of weaver's loom
spinning enchanting rainbow web.

Rest in the square on sun-toasted bench,
savouring creamy chocolate ice,
summoning strength to immerse my limbs
in Lisdoonvarna's waters.

Honeysuckle days float
in a haze of billowing heady hawthorn,
earthbound cares sail away
in clear running streams of skylark's song.

The lark must eventually come back to earth
to forage to feed its young
and I must return through the noise and speed
to the workaday world at home.

But I find that horizons have opened my eyes
to the space and the length
and the height and the depth
of the wonder of simple things.

I see the smile on the upturned face
of the daisies on my lawn
and my spirits climb with the honeysuckle vine
as I drink of the neighbour's hawthorn.

Oonagh Twomey

Corsica

The land it stronger than the people
It wraps itself around you
Holding, until all the pain is gone.
Only the purity of strength is left
Caressing, that you would know its depths.

Jackie Draysey

For Elliot

My love is a child in the remembering night
Who dances the numbered face of my head
And ticks an orbit of my thoughts
To time me a sadness forever
Through this life-long landscape so isolate
Where I trundle my old heart around,
Dead weight and gravely blistered.
Intrepid wings away on a blue note.

My time locates a long lonely moment
And weighs the hours into immortal years.
Tears roll eternal down my face.

All my passion speaks of devils,
Stirring something way past wicked,
Loading tongues of evils;
Powering the force and fullness of life
This passion is the presence of others within;
And though I loathe I love to long,
All my loosely ticking time,

To hold you among sticks and bad coughs
At odd hours of the winsome day.

M Whitecross

'White Squall' - Marina - And The Sea

We sit
Still on an azure sea
Embraced by rugged hills
Like many eyes gazing
Square windows in white boxes
Watch over us

Bleached wood
Bronzed sailors
Bare feet
Tortola sun
Marina of the 'White Squall'
Queen of the Sea
Sits by the wheel
Looking out
Wishing to be gone

Now dips her bows
In coloured water
Raises her head
In joyful glee
'White Squall' is happy
She is free

Captain Fred at the stern
Proud as a figurehead
Gently rocking
In tune with the elements
'White Squall' forges on

Painted clouds
Above treasure islands
Deep blue seas
Unfurled sail
Happy voices raised in chorus
Splashing
Through the tumbling foam
Laughter
Echoes a happy day

While we day-trip sailors
Only sail her in our dreams
Our waking thoughts
Will always be
With 'White Squall'
Marina - and the sea

Norma Walker

Jolly Joe

When days are full of worry
and your life is full of strife,
come listen to the one man band
and have the time of your life.
When you need a break,
now the jobs are done
and your mind is in a spin,
come listen to the one man band,
make a loud and terrible din.
With a crash, crash, crash
and a thump, thump, thump,
you begin to tap your toe
and everybody in our town,
comes to hear old Jolly Joe.
Now you'll jig along,
to an old sweet song,
that he's played for many years.
For the one man band,
makes a special sound,
that will fill your eyes with tears.
Jolly Joe gives joy to the world,
he greets us all as friends
and in his music you will find,
this message which he sends:
Love one another,
never hurt a fly
and when you're grey and very old,
your memories will not die.

Tom Clarke

Summer Wine

Lying on the ground with the grass so dry,
I get sleepy with the smell, as flies go by.
Intoxicating aura from the deep red wine
As I roll it in my mouth and feel fine.

The sun dancing on my glass,
Its light wiping shadows from my mind.
Basking in the warmth I delight
And drink my deep, my deep, red, red wine.

Dry earth has a fragrance that strokes my senses
Floating in the heady air, calming my defences.
The wind ruffles patterns in the hair on my head
Makes ripples 'pon the surface of the wine that is red.

The sun dancing on my glass,
Its light wiping shadows from my mind.
Basking in the warmth I delight
And drink my deep, my deep, red, red wine.

I'm surrounded and contained by the wild,
Lonely inside nature not yet defiled.
My thoughts wander through centuries, along miles of road.
Basking in the warm I delight and drink
My deep, my deep, red Summer wine.
Drinking wine all the way yet not drowning.
Not drowning 'cept in the grass, wind and sun.

Laura Sherlock

The Fall Of A Boxer

In the ring he danced with the wind neath his feet
swift and alert no fear of defeat
His knockdown punch floored many a foe
and the audience roared, a magnificent show.

The fame made him happy embracing the glory
an end never near, this was his dream story
Never a loser his fitness top peak
friends gathered round, week after week.

Popular and confident, a drink now and then
another drink, a party, these were good friends
His fitness diminished, co-ordination lost
respect slowly vanished, his marriage the cost.

Breakdown and sadness, with no place to rest
in a bar he slept, his bed and breakfast
People glance and look away
forgetful of his power in the glory days.

They see a man inebriated, forgetting his past
when they followed the boxer, and relished his cast
But he remembers through red misty eyes
when he could have been king, his name in the skies.

Though easily led and a taste for strong wine
boasting in company of conquests through time
They leave him alone and he talks to the air
unknowing, too stupored, that no-one is there.

He covers his face with his fist stance and beams
he is still a boxer, if only in dreams.

Jacquie Williams

Retreat To Valdemosa

Chopin was magic, all fineness,
nerves like electric wires, manic;
he cared what the neighbours would say,
their wagging tongues put him in a panic.

George was butch but didn't know it,
wanted to storm the Male Domain,
beat them at their own game; she gave
Fred, like the rest, a bad time of it in the main.

Yet this time of it, joy and pain
was what came out in the notes,
those mad mazurkas, lilting polonaises,
triste nocturnes, pure nerve stretched thin as coats

of paint over feeling close to the bone:
and she, mistaking her true forte,
indifferent to the gossipers next door
but timid that Beau Monde taste might find her naughty,

whilst giving herself to passion, sometimes,
could, of herself, give nothing more,
wrote in a clipped chaste style about the flora
and fauna, voluminously, a 19th Century Thomson's Tour,

denying her feelings. Did she feel a thing?
Maybe she thought he, with his soul so bared,
his heart so exposed, has feeling enough for us both.
For that kind of thing only a little time could be spared.

Meanwhile summer and autumn and winter
journals one after the other flowed,
forgotten, worthy and vast unread,
tomes from the dead; yet her portrait showed

a face in repose, trusting and tender,
that might, with luck and courage, have learned to love:
a lass, what she was, human, vulnerable,
for Frederic's sighing line to be worthy of.

Peter Dean

Made With Hands

Paraphrasing Pater
I am older than the chair
On which I sit,
That is, on this, not that one.

Man the maker
Is seldom coeval
With the things he makes.
Longer or shorter lasting
Size is no rule,
The smallest often lasts the longest:
Vessels and ornaments or artefacts
End archaeologically or drowned in seas
Yet buildings are destroyed in a youth's span.

Obsolescence is a concept
But chance or natural force
Can end a thing as well.
The overlapping of those spans and ours
Embodied by the things still with us
That came before
So many generations
Set up the echoes of involvement
In a stop-watched race of time.

H Massy

Ambush

December chill upon the air
Iron-hard ground, the trees almost bare.
The small urban garden an oasis of calm
Cold-weather chattering of birds keeping warm
Sheltering in bushes, awaiting their turn
To feed at the table, bathe in the pool
The quarrelsome starlings the noisiest of all.

The bush-lined garden offers protection from cold
Concealed in the branches, birds timid and bold.
A prowling cat picks her way along a wall
All eyes are upon her, she stands no chance at all
Of catching a bird or playing her games
The best she can hope for are bird table remains.

A small dashing hawk, hunting on the wing
Her movements controlled, her judgement unerring
Skimming the bushes, silent and low
Searching her subject from the cover below.
She selects her victim and without further delay -
Striking in surprise attack, she swoops on unsuspecting prey.

A momentary stunned silence, then raucous alarm
Rises up from the bushes as realisation dawns.
Ignoring the upset, she crouches below
Jealously guarding with mantled wings
Working fast to rip plumage, before rising in flight
Bearing her prize, won with skill and no fight.

The chattering panic continues long after she has gone
The starling numbers now lessened brutally by one.
Of the hapless victim, there's nothing to be found
Save for the soft, speckled feathers littering the ground.

Joy Saunders

Final Hour

Too far for echo, secret on the hill-top,
The fated castle, further than wrath or music,
First lodge to strangeness and to dreams' beginning;
And must we go as far as that far castle?

And must we find it too, a witless ruin,
Walled-in and brooding in a nightmare sleep?
Delicate dreams still haunt this outpost building,
Gable and garden still some quiet keep . . .

Or do we haunt it, at the lintel standing,
With image conjured from that distant vision,
Awakened by its presence, and foreboding
That we have leagues to journey ere we slumber?

Leagues there are yet to travel without number,
And we must on our way, and leave this brooding
House on the edge of day.

Elsa Ivor

Getting Ready

In a time not too distant
I'll come here no more
To pass through your
Constantly welcoming door.

Don't fret for me then
As I can't for me now,
And I'll go not unhappy,
Though, just tired of it all,
Take one small fey last bow.

Please;
No rite and no ritual,
No sad final roll,
No societal itchings
In the back of your soul,
For I'll irritate
No-one I loved anymore.

So;
If some warm summer night
You spy me in your dreams,
Then smile for me gently
Or give maybe a wave
And I'll not be a shade
Where you need be afraid.

Jim Rogerson

By Instalments

Discount Saturday.
South East somewhere.

Barefoot black girl.
Corner shop bound.
Travelling retail.
Her . . . never never land.

Standing order on life.
Pays by instalments.

Today she must choose.
Something for tea . . .

Or the luxury of shoes?

D I Ross

The Tiger

The tiger in her ivory tower
So far removed from worldly power
A satin finish she desires infact
Hopeless is her rage intact
A burden for some within a fact.

Few could touch upon her beauty
Harshness piled her lonesome poetry
A world alone forever be
The tiger in her.

She moves with grace, alone, apart
Impossible task to find her heart
I'd give my all, to comfort all
The torture force, she stores so tall
Impenetrable she will remain
The tiger in her.

George Livingston Shand

Monday Night

Monday night in the ghost-town capital,
A student and a lone parent looking for the exotic,
It's cold outside and empty inside
But plenty of lights show what's on offer.

New club with futuristic name beckons, entices,
Sounds like something from a Sci-fi film;
As number seven comes up on a gaming machine
The screen offers a chance at luck.

And all the workers with the readies
Don't go out until the weekend's call
But it's OK for all the others;
They have freedom to go and catch the night.

Oasis predictably preaching echoes of the Fab Four,
Taking over minds of the nation's numb;
Heroes of the dispossessed blare in glare of bar-room,
If you know what I mean?

Steve Andrews

Lodore Falls

By day and night it runs
Ceaselessly -
Snaking down through clefted rock
Roaring over polished stone
Hurrying always, as if there is no time
Not even for walkers who attempt the climb.

Ever fierce Lodore Falls
Ever Swift and deep
Yet also the picture of content
Winding your way through green banks
And chattering still, until the deep descent -
Continuous and True
The inspiration for a poet's thoughts
Springing from you.

Rachel Gallehawk

The Till Lady

Julie Johnson worked a till
And gradually, against her will
She fell in lust, with John McKay,
Who came to shop there every day.

One bright morning, with a wink,
He asked her out to have a drink.
'Please come,' he whispered, 'Please!' He cried,
So to her husband, Sam, she lied.

'My friend is dead,' she phoned to Sam.
'I'm going to comfort her old mam.'
'Oh dear!' Said Sam, 'Don't fret for me,
I'll just go home and make my tea.'

That night they had the finest time,
John drank whiskey, she drank wine
And when the night drew to a close,
He handed her a single rose.

Next day, Sam met the friend who'd 'died'
And realising she had lied
Confronting Mrs Johnson, said,
'I thought you said your friend was dead!'

Julie, open-mouthed, just gazed
The shock had left her in a daze.
She couldn't think of what to do
But Sam could, and he told her too!

'I think I'll wall you up,' he'd laugh,
'Or, maybe drown you in the bath,
Or hang you from the old oak tree,
Or chop you up! Sounds good to me.'

In a flash, she grabbed a knife
And with one stab she took Sam's life,
Then buried him out in the lea,
And told the world he'd gone to sea.

She went to live with lover John,
Who was well pleased that Sam had gone.
He tended to her every whim
Delighted, that she'd turned to him.

Julie Johnson works a till,
And one spring day, against her will,
She fell in lust, with Michael Ray,
Who comes to shop there every day.

Felicity Griffiths

Trails

The dream mountain beckons me
and once there I will be immortal,
refined . . .
No longer an outsider, but a real totem.
I will have feathers,
claws,
silver jaws,
bright red eyes.
But, most of all,
Everything?

Sweetwater being replaced by smartwater
may my shape be outlined in the canyons
and never remembered with scorn.
Outlived but never outlasted.
Gotten long in the tooth lost in the eye of this war,
and nearing the close of darkness,
you were resurrected.
And at your side you made me
everything.

D Manning

. . . *Legend*

History will remember,
the years in which you dominated our lives.
Whatever was said,
it will not deter.
Legend.

Yesterday will be rejoiced,
and your true meaning will become clear.
Whatever she said,
will not matter.
Legend.

A partnership lasts forever,
even the fifteen clubs each day.
Whatever he said,
sing a lullaby.
Legend.

Richard Westwood

For The Crop To Ripen

But for a shadow of what was,
In prisoners shackles bound,
The plight of freedom was a crime,
Thirty years of life entered into a vacuum.

The benefits yet have to ripen,
Fruits of salvation soon to be harvested,
Mouths water to the taste of freedom.

No wind can ruin the crop,
Many hands to render it,
Freedoms crop is sown deep,
Weather cannot help the tyrant.

Niall O Ceallaigh

A Child's Trick

When you are in the bath, take a bar of soap.
And take a bar of water, then mix them in your hand.
Scrunch the forefinger into the curve of the thumb,
Without an opening, and then create one.

Where there should be nothing, there will be something;
Invisible, save under the light, the oily film is an
Indefinably definite barrier - for what is it but a sheen?
A miniature rainbow, strung between digits.

Breathe on it softly, and the colours eddy and swirl,
Blow on it gently, and it grows greater, to become a bubble;
The same and yet changed at once, for where there was a plane
There is now an inside and an outside.

The illusion is very fragile;
Separate the fingers, the window will shatter,
Blow too hard, the sphere will pop,
And even left to itself, it will fade away.

Scientists may seek to explain it with their ions,
Poets may transcend it with their metaphors,
But here, now, I am no poet, no scientist;
I am a man in the bath, playing with soap and water.

Perhaps that is the trick.

William Tabraham

The Pebbles' Song

Great waves
breaking over pebbles.
Gleaming beads
sucked back,
flung up
on the beach
and each
cries 'I'.
Pulled back,
thrust forward
and colliding
there's a song
waiting to be sung
in each one.
Look closely,
you can see
the seas notation
written on it.
The sea shells surge
a song, too.
A haunting rush
leading the way
to stillness
and some greater symphony.

Peter Bentley

The Source

Deep, within the darkest depths -
singing softly to herself;
curious to see the outside world,
she pushes herself from pure beginnings

thro' - rock - gushing over the crevices;
trickling thro' cracks in the centuries-old layers.
Pulsating. Bubbling; until at last she
raises her pure face to the outer air.

Sometimes, coming up on snow clad slopes.
Most times, on bare rock face,
then joyously, a trickle at first,
she makes her tentative way thro'
the roughest terrain.

A crystal tear gleams in the sun -
becomes a small stream; joined by
another - and yet another.
Then, this concentration of purity finds

a deep ravine. Joyously, trustingly,
plunges over in a waterfall of crystal hair.
An Ice maiden, proudly showing off
her sparkling beauty.

Bouncing now over rocks, frothing, foaming,
showing lacy petticoats this miss
dances thro' a valley, flirting with
the mossy banks, throwing a kiss to

a passing dragonfly, bejewelled in the sun.
'Come, my pretty one, come,' she seems to croon.
Swirling more darkly now, as the earth torn from
new banks tumble into her once pristine depths -
still - she smiles for she knows how essential
she is to man.

Gleeful children toss pebbles, laughing to see
the ever widening circles.
Men lounge contentedly. Pipe between their teeth,
rods propped up in front hopefully.

Women in pretty frocks gaze into her depths
breathing 'Isn't it beautiful?'
Still murmuring to herself, she wends purposefully
to her intended place in the scheme of things.
The wide and azure sea.

Fuchsia Coles

Flowing Tresses

Long flowing tresses seek to embellish the shapely shoulder blades.
Soft blonde locks silkily sheen in the high summer's coolest glades.
The wild wind playfully teases wisps to waft most delicately about.
Such a beautiful mane of golden strands is a certainty to stand out!

Brushed and lacquered with loving care they perfumed the very air.
Many heads turned at the heavenly sight to feast on a picture so fair.
Doors opened wide, all stepped aside, a parting of the great Red Sea.
Such flouncing waves caused mighty raves as all fell upon one
knee.
Admired from near and envied from afar, rare jewels of wild
delight,
Gracing the evening's pillow case to unfurl, a truly precious sight,
Glittering, shimmering, aping most delicate threads of purest
gold,
To frame the most glorious picture that one ever wished to
behold.

As years flowed by they matured to flourish, still a captivating
sigh.
Many tried to imitate their hue from costly ampoules of various
dye.
Television homages to their curator were flashed daily across the sky.
Alas, the rarest specimen in a soup tureen, floods the discerning
eye.

T Burke

61

Beauty And The Earth Man

Moved with your chattering.
Above the ear of giants
in canopy's of peace, remote.
Arise - man.
Touch but a grin.
Let us elope to shores of varied kind
Of love, of dance, of wine.
And even as we speak soft rains
would fall.
Monuments of magic, cascades of echo'd
beauty decadent.
Unarmed allowing all.
Sweet nostalgic streets
ablaze and busy, like remote's opposing
face.
Now measure, mark, inflict on those you love
this masterpiece of fresh exciting passion.

Anthony M L Williams

The Visitor's Here

Silently I arrived an itinerant hitch-hiker with virus unknown,
Slowly manifesting to a stage where rampant I have grown,
From this vast expanse of universe I have travelled,
With this killer that as yet your scientists have not unravelled,

A germ I could be called one let loose from outer space,
With genetic form a blueprint to wipe out the whole human race,
Some of your modern day diseases are just the start,
Of this the very essence of which I am a part,

When your rockets and space probes forged the way for mankind,
Little did you know what else out there you would find,
Steadily working our way from the galaxies for there are more than
me,
Unnameable terminators that being invisible none can see,

Predator on the prowl an alien dare one could say,
Out there you could be host even as you read this today,
From deep within some black hole our army emerges free,
So if you feel ill tonight remember to think of me.

Ann G Wallace

Disney's Dream

Walt Disney had so many
eggs in his basket, I

call it talent not luck;
sure if Mickey Mouse hadn't

been the King in his hand,
he had an Ace up his sleeve

called Donald Duck.

James Sherman

We Will Be Laid

We will be laid
in beds of soil;
a bird will sing,
grass will cry,
black beetles will kneel on our faces,
praying for us to God

Gregory Baczewski

Ant In Amber

Well? you knew - it's done, she's gone. You knew well
the glass bead game you chanced, beholden
in her trance, fixed in sticky love - golden
amber love. You, an ancient insect, fell,
honey fool! Fell into her syrup cell.
Those carved, gleaming streams enslaved, enfolding,
sucking down and in - wrapped, enrapt, moulding
you - you fool - inside her hardening shell.

Yes, she fossil-fused you in her glass-coat
trap - in her vitrified indifference -
sealed you in a bubble - you specimen!

So now you're in a bead about her throat,
latest on the string, a reassurance
of the past to be fingered now and then.

Seán Holden

What Is The Cross For You ?

The cross for me
Is times past,
Hurts still not healed
That I may not yet put down.
Memories of violence
In words and actions,
Criticism unjustly
Knocking nails into me.
Never knowing
From childhood
The security of love,
Believing to gain it
I must be good.
Fear then my companion
For as long as I can recall,
A feeling of lostness
Life out of control,
Unworthiness at just being me.

Kath McGowan.

The Spirits Of The Standing Stones

Across the corn fields, crops and chalk
Night closes tight the door to day,
Stars stud the skies which watch us walk
While phantoms rise from where they lay,
To float beyond the scope of eyes
Where human senses cannot reach,
Beneath bright mystic Wiltshire skies
And tangled roots of ancient beech.

What stones are these, stood proud, sublime,
Where thistles spear the sunlit hours,
Do they remember now the time
When first they graced the grass and flowers?
A breeze is bouncing by old posts
Designed to keep the people out,
But not the eerie Wiltshire ghosts
Which haunt at night and float about.

White moon! Above this grassy hill,
Sail through the spirits where now moans
The nakedness of the night whose chill
Soaks now the silence of these stones,
It pools upon the Earth to seep
Into its chasms and the womb,
Where those forgotten, stray and sleep
  Deep in some subterranean tomb.

Nicholas Winn

Appliances

Paula and I were in Tandy or Dixons
on Ken High Street looking for one
of those plugs to fix my answering machine
and they were playing this 70s soulful
music with this raspy man's voice singing
about the way he loved his baby
and what he was going to do to her
that night. And Paula said:
'When I hear songs like this
I really wish someone
loved me like that.'

I never thought I'd start looking old.
I never thought I'd know what she meant.

R Soames

The Brown Tweed Jacket

The brown tweed jacket
It hangs beneath the stairs
Many times I've tried to take it down
But every time I've failed
So many memories, so many tears
Wait; I tell my broken heart
Those memories were not all sad
Don't throw it away, be glad
Jim wore that jacket, when he was well

See him now walking tall
A gentleman, taking a walk
His dog, a faithful pal, trotting alongside
Jim whistling a tune, taking long strides
Happy times indeed, can't they last forever

No, but those memories can
So leave the jacket in its place
Look at it from time to time
Think of Jim and smile
Be Happy for just awhile.

Wyn Burdett-Conlan

In Memoriam For CB

Bright sun, a chilling wind, and
       A sweet scent of death -
This day draws us together
       At your going. Goodbye is
Too easy a word, but true, here.
       Too briefly you stayed,
       Where now your last breath
Meets ours on the ruffling breeze.
       But you have been found.
       We who have lost you
Lost by you more than we knew
       Or could understand,
And now wait poised on the edge of
Our lives, see nothing outside
       Cypresses that hedge
The graveyard.
       Words are so hard,
They come tapping on the mind's
Window, pointing the way we
       Would rather not go.
Easier to stay safe behind
The pane, protesting we see.

We came to your death as though
To a great door slammed shut. Yet you
       Gave one light push and
It opened easily, to
Admit an expected guest.
All you were is gathered up
Into a new day, now you've drained
       Your last bitter cup.

Our cars file off down the drive
       By newly-dug graves.
What do we take with us past
       The gate? - A lack where
You were, a crack in the glass
Glittering from that daylight
       Where you go.
              We stay.
This empty space you leave here
       Grows to a living place.

David Moorcroft

A Few Home Truths

I mow the carpet
and vacuum the lawn,
I keep up the struggle
from dusk until dawn.

I cook the clothes
and iron the dinner,
the rest of the family's
now very much thinner.

I'll polish the linen
and spin dry a shoe,
as for home economies
I haven't a clue.

I can poach an ice-cream
and freeze a whole egg,
I can't cook for toffee
so I might as well beg.

I will oil the children
and spoon feed the car,
to plan all the shopping
I'll never get far.

I programme the ceiling
the video I plaster,
my do it yourself
is a complete disaster.

I pay the rubbish
and empty the rent,
I think I will go
and live in a tent!

Mark Peacey

West From Skaigh

I stand before your ancient barrenness,
boulder strewn, soft moorland;
unfolding your stark beauty
against an empty sky;

in water you're renewed,
green and sparkled in your gown;
girdled grey in drystone walls,
snug within a cloak of mists;

bathed in sunshine, yet cut,
by cruellest edge of winters knife;
where heather dances in the wind
beneath the moon mute Tors.

Steve Newbury

C'Driscoll Castle

Rustling of ivied stones
of uncertain centuries,
their memories in heap
buttressing their past.

Unpaned windows mirroring
ghosts of yesteryear,
peering at ever changing sea
and men building endeavours.

Aloft imaginary thatch
birds glide, imperturbed,
then a shriek, a caw,
diving thru' unhinged doors.

G P B

My Numb Hand

Sleeping on my hand at half past two,
Sleeping on my hand in morning dew,
Fingers feel a lifeless dump;
Chin hair rubs an ice cold lump.

The morning runs but the hand in danger -
Victim of forced slave rule,
Of when to move and when to lose -
No consultation for dead strangers.
No consolation for still hand's friends.

One moment's assumed reflex
Wiped out in dark surprise,
Fingers finished dancing,
Never allowed wave good-bye;
No more to greet or cry.

Part II
Joy

Sudden movements scare the remainder;
Dancing fingers crawl and breed,
Fight back doomed destiny!
Surprised by surprise, relieved by joy,
Rise to appreciate this second chance,
Romancing at new life-line thrown;
Flowing again to live and let write.

Vincent P Martin

Reflections On Freedom

My heart bleeds for the caged bird
I panic whenever I look at him
I cannot bear his captivity
So akin to my own
Nobody will free either of us,
It is assumed he has never known freedom
Therefore he could not survive,
I shall remain 'caged' because a part of me
Is desperately afraid of failure.
How carelessly I discarded my freedom
Let it fall from my shoulders like a superfluous wrap,
Nobody warned me of the impending suffocation
The beating of frantic wings against the glass -
The cry of my own insufficiency
I take refuge in images of Dingle
Racing barefoot along endless white sands
Intoxicated by sea birds soaring above me
Clasping the blessed gift to my aching heart.

Gabrielle Whyte

Waterlogged

What happened to the self
I was before I came here?
Comb for it on the beach
On a long, wet world of sand.
Look out to sea and what was
The infinity of you and me.
Now what do you see?
No one. No more you, no more me, only
Wriggling coils, spiralling in the air.
Life now underground, like on Mars,
Nowhere to go, surface bare,
Only worm whorls disturbed by a toe,
Bare, numb, cold, disrupting the flow
Of whirlpools in a worthless void.
Ectomorphic burial,
Ectoplasm of organisms now entombed
Under avalanche of old time.
Whose time? Certainly not yours or mine.
Tread in the gophers,
Leave footprints in soak of sand
As I reach out for your hand
Through a quagmire of ideas,
Beliefs, hopes, fears,
Once wild wilderness of wet desires
I touch only a morass of mud, monophobia, madness
In this swamp of despair.
Float me up to the light, life there
Fill in my footprints, your trace,
Before the tide sweeps in, obliterates
Our love, and drowns my tear stained face.

Heather Bruyère Watt

A Blurb On New Blood

A suck of brainbloodwords
sustains me with my weekly fix
            of metaphor.

I strive for that slick lick
of innovation.

I've hitched a ride on motion
& birds waved wings
to salute audacity.

A youngblood's
broodingbraideddeathwords
trigger a transition
of synapse trailthoughts
spiderwebbing transformation.

I've seen an artisan exotic
swirling in her finery
announce her presence
with dignified silence
but when she spoke
she spun her cloth of verse
stating the purpose of her craft.
About egos & dissension
powerlust & criticisms
she stated calmly -
'I must create.'

A twist/a slant/a curve or two
upon threadbared clichés
alters the mural
we all occupy.

   Carmen M Pursifull

Feline Humphrey Of No 10

(I dedicate this poem to the Royal Society for the Prevention of Cruelty to Animals.)

Roadworn, pawsore, cold, hungry, and longing for attention,
Three year old moggie of no fixed abode, sans affection,
Braving children's stones, and the yipping insults of housedogs,
Head low, with an occasional look to the side, he plods,
Stepping lightly and painfully in the tracks of Downing Street,
Stealthily sneaking to the Cabinet Office for retreat,
Much to the delight of the Staff who took to him kindly,
Naming him after Hawthorne's Civil Servant, as Humphrey.
Soon emboldened, Humphrey moves to adjacent Number Ten
Roaming these two Offices, and splitting time between them!
Unimpaired monarch of all he surveyed, Humphrey became,
And with none his right to dispute, he rocketed to fame
Predominantly as Number Ten's Supreme Mouse-Catcher,
Beginning with the era of Premier Margaret Thatcher:
In ninety, Thatcher moved, but Humphrey decided to stay;
Major re-elected - Humphrey hangs on - but starts to stray:
Just as his big brother, the Leopard, cannot change its spots,
Humphrey's display of his animal instincts never stops!
He transgressed his bounds killing two Robins and a Duckling,
And hitched a ride in a Mail Van and returned trembling!
Once, being mistakenly reported 'Dead' in the Times,
Was later featured on Cabinet Christmas Cards with chimes!
Just as Prime Ministers come and go serving terms in Office,
The Blair Era spelt Humphrey's doom after eleven years service:
Rocketing from obscurity under three Prime Ministers,
And life span in human terms, attaining seventy seven years,
Being disabled by incontinent and kidney inertia,
Is retired from hectic Whitehall to a suburbia,
Sans any Votes Of Thanks, or Last Lament, or Eulogia!

Welch Jeyaraj Balasimgam

For I Am But A Passer-By (In a vast vast crowd)

I lie here in my broken dreams, and silently cry within my mind,
I hear the artists gain their pleasure, from interaction and off beat
                                                            leisure,
Or sit and watch a vast vast crowd, that's prettily arranged like
                                                            flowers,
But I, I am but a passer by, far too lost to be part of a crowd,
I have lost my mind for a long long while, been broken by life's
                                                            awful cards,
Alone in my ghostly shadows, not a whisper, not a sound, just those
                                                            actors lines,
There's a tune deep within my soul,
It plays a little Mozart melody, don't you know.
I hope to reveal it to the Lord, one day,
But I, I am but a passer by, a torn and tattered fragile man,
That no-one can really understand.
Yes I, I am just a passer by, broken by life's awful attire.

Tom Maltby

Father

Your love protected and kept me safe,
within your make-believe world.
But you removed that love,
and taught me hate.
Nearly drowning me
within a sea of harsh reality.

Nuressa Bessell

To A Lass

Our moor and mountain
Our spirits soar
The eyes sparkle with anticipation
The smile widens
The body trembles
Morning dew beckons the naked foot
Heather springs to touch
Waterfall tumbling, vibrating our souls.
We are as one as the eagle soars in
    the bursting sun.

Jim Bennett

Uncatchable Clouds

Silently painted by the king in the sky
Shaped and blown by the wind.
Heaven?
As good as.
My Heaven.
My physical body reaches not far enough
Into this miracle.
But my mind soars,
Like an Angel finding home at last.

Breathing and feeling,
Time
As it flows
Into every corridor of my mind.
Conquering space in my spirit.

Within the clouds of truth I play
Ageless I become,
But cannot stay.
When I return no face will know
Where I've been,
Except, another soul like me.

Lisa-Anne Shirley

Dreaming

In a dream I walked with you,
Through misty meadows where
Light morning dew glistened with the birth of day.
And your smile radiated warmth
Before the sun reluctantly rose
Through the night's black and cold
To replace the stars once more.
But as I woke, I realised you were gone;
The sun has no reason
To try to warm my heart,
And the stars seem as distant and lost
As you are to me now.
And all I can do
Is wait for sleep to come and take me.
Finally, when the stars explode with brilliance,
All of this will play across your face,
Where my hand will reach to touch the tears,
And we can dream together for eternity.

Kirsty Burge

A Sad Song

Her life is like the saddest song
a dark and mournful tune
the lyrics full of things gone wrong
sang beneath the bluest moon

Her home is like a tomb inside
she sits in silent grief
prodding wounds still open wide
refusing comfort or relief.

Her beauty shows an autumn fade
summer smiles escape no more
her nature's now for winter made
and spring will bring no thaw.

Her lips are thin and set and cold
no more will they be kissed
no more will she know passions hold
and little is it missed.

It's love that broke her heart you see
betrayed her in her prime
he took the best, then fled to sea
and chose to marry maritime.

Terry Adams

Untitled

A warm wave washes over me
and time slowly erodes the tiny granules of sand
from underneath my body
taking away my fears
and dissolving my hopes
and dreams
I sink down
further and further
into the depths of oblivion
away from life
and I cleanse my soul

Melinda Best

Sonnet

For a lady whose favourite vase was broken.

The fragile vase lies broken in the hearth;
you kneel to pick the pieces, and may ask
if sorrow needs to be the aftermath
of so much loveliness; may you not bask
in beauty all your living loving years,
safe from the darkened days that caused you tears;
they tell you time will heal, but time will tell;
though mended, vase and heart show scars as well.

But close your fingers fast, and clutching hard
over a fragment, as the shining shard
lies locked within the prison of your palm,
safe from the world, and hid from further harm,
the perfect image rests, pure and apart,
within the magic mirror of your heart.

Chris Goodwin

In A Different Saturday Night

With the night caught in my hair
And my best clothes
Absorbing the coldness of his eyes,
I stood between Saturday Night
And Sunday Morning,
Where the dancing ends, music dies,
Waiting on some unseen incendiary
To cause
The midnight sun to rise.

Watching lovers twisted like vines
Around promises of desire,
Ascending heavenwards as I faced home
Like a momentary grimace
Outside a universe of bliss:
Sons of Adam, Daughters of Eve
Engaged in a universal kiss,
Heaven and earth coming closer than ever
And love descending in reflections,
Disappearing into the concrete
Hardening beneath our feet.

This is the peaceful hour
Where absence knows no cure
And the neutral stars
Are close enough to possess
But I want the quiet hour,
Deliverance from the
Infernal mess
Of my head
And a thwarted love
Fortune will not bless.

Paula Morris

Two Swans

I was sitting on the beach,
With the wind in my face.

I was glad to be here,
Happy to be away.

I like looking at the sea,
And looking at the sky,
And high above two swans passed by.

I first saw her,
As she came,
Walking close to the shore.

This slim young girl,
Wearing a long blue dress.

Oblivious to the world,
She was lost in herself.

It was too late for tears,
Her childhood was gone.

She stopped.
She turned,
She walked into the sea.

Then with her dress all wet,
She just stood there,
Staring down,
At one hand in the water.

And for two swans on high,
What do they care?
They've seen this before.

I wanted to reach out,
And touch her,
But she was too far away.

She saw me,
And just looked;
A face without emotion.

Crossing her arms to hide her breast,
She started running.
Everything taken away,
In one savage act.

After she'd gone,
I turned back to the sky.

Completely useless.

And I watched two swans eclipse the sun.

Stuart Boyd

What God

You've heard the street talking
about our love.
And that's why
we're introverted tonight.
And, for the rest of our lives.
What God
has put us under!
No rhyme, nor tongues
pouring scandal will divide.

One furtive morning, misconstrued by
the lazy ones,
I grew, into a pillar of salt.
Lonelier than Jezebel in the Bible.
What God
has looked upon as joy between
two lonely lovers
has hurt me.

You've heard from your friends
about me.
What God shares
has come quietly now:
Thrown, our hearts into the trash,
forever.

Kirk Watson

Babel

Unknown characters on a page
keep secrets of continents;
fascinating up and downstrokes
tell of tragedy and achievement
to the initiated.
But as surely as a locked door
the strange words keep mother-tongued
strangers out.
We stare helplessly at shapes
which have a greater significance
than mere squiggles on paper.
The exploits of El Cid
reside among the pages
of Spanish literature
but are mute when
other tongued linguists look
but do not see.
Translators help - or hinder?
After surgery, the patient is not the same
and we long to know the fate of Aramaic, Hebrew, Greek
after Experts with lexicons have had their way.

Leonard Saunders

Where Are The Angels?

The neutrality of sleep, its resistance to tortured time,
Is lost to the racing mind, paradoxical to the minute like an hour,
What is that lamp for, that book, that paper all hugged by
                                                    normality?
Transported by this unreal schism away from a normality so
                                                    desperately desired,
No escape from this unfettered, malignant, omnipotent power,
Where are the angels?

Good days (and goodnights) with inhalations of spirit, only peaceful,
In their relativity to a suffocating miasma of unlubricated thought,
Like those on a sunlit bus of the presence of a 5th dimensional
                                                    darkness outside,
And of what worth has a life with death where a billion chemicals
                                                    decay,
That personal recycled concoction of existence irretrievably ending in
                                                    nought,
Where are the angels?

Long, long walks down tunnels with emaciated walls of horror,
Pushed on by feelings of inhabiting a warped and sepia-pictured
                                                    nadir,
Abandoned, so abandoned with not only clothes but skin also
                                                    stripped,
To the bone, a bone in the ground, unthinking, dirty forgotten,
Of a body disorientated, scraped and mutilated by fear,
Where are the angels?

A room with four corners, a bed to crouch on, in one corner to back
                                                    into,
(Not sleep), away, above of menacing flatland below, a view
                                                    of the door,
A view abdicated with eyes down, open yet closed, with bars of
                                                    air like a cage,
Put on the lamp, put on the light, diffuse these molecules that
                                                    grip,
But only a recording of a crushing embrace, psyche
                                                    crumbling to the core,
Where are the angels?

A daytime, a night-time, equally wretched in the paint of a cosmic
                                                    blackness,
A colour of inexplicable aura pointing fingers, inaccessible to
                                                    those painless,
Demonic digits shimmer in and out of inner space but forever
                                                    there,
Real hands are clenched and unclenched, nails dig deep into real
                                                    flesh,
In slavery to a diabolical parallel universe with an infinity of
                                                    madness,
Oh God, if you exist, where are your Angels?

   Brett Purlee

Distant Cousins

How grim it was to see how much they'd changed,
Marred by their march through twenty testing years!
Once youthful wags had grown a mite deranged,
And carefree girls a touch too prone to tears.
No doubt I was assessed the same sad way
By wary men who shared a joyless grin;
Scorned as that dolt with hair and dreams gone grey,
By former sirens sporting chin on chin.
Then there she was! The smile was just the same!
The eyes, the grace; she had not aged at all!
Heart stopped, throat closing, I breathed soft her name.
Why held she not the whole wide world in thrail?
I'd wondered that full twenty years before,
And still they all proved blind in what I saw!

John M Coutts

Eclipsing Canute

One day I will go out and walk
      into the sea,
with no flatterers to protect me
nor habit to hinder me,
and the breakers will break their
      fists
on my chin
and the scrimmaging foam will try
      in vain
to wrestle and rock me down;

and horizons that pushed me back
will give way to my surging,
and the beasts of the sea will flee
      in a frenzy
of flashing tails and darting fins,
whales and dolphins and squid
vying with cuttlefish scuttling
scared back into their sleepy deep,
as the seabed itself rises to greet
      my king's step
and the waters part.

No shell or stone will worry my
      tread,
only the soft ground soundless pith,
the millennial stirrings of dead
      Vikings
drowned under mountainous waves,
will powder my path,
their chalk-light sandals pledged
      to me,
when I go out and walk into the sea.

John Ellis

The Seashore

On sunny sand I rest my head
Beside the clear blue sea,
Which swells and heaves,
Yet gently laps a song,
As breakers surf upon the shore,
To ripple all along the bay,
A sweeping arc that softly ends,
Where water kisses day.

I must depart from this sweet cove,
    Away from palm-lined shore,
Away from love here interwove,
    Though not for evermore!
For I shall come to you again,
    Beside this lovely sea;
As then the battle will be won,
    And then I shall be free!

Paul Butters

Laser

Light establishes and decorates the world,
Streaming through Creation since the huge beginning,
Legions of lucidity awakening a foam of lives
On planetary shores into our microscopic dawn;
Developing the eye's bright sense to see itself
Resplendent in the suns of morning's fresco;
Arching over ocean's shimmering manifold its rainbow promise,
As Apollo's golden chariot traversing mythic skies,
In a visionary flash by whips of loosened lightning's
Making manifest the white, electric anger of the gods,

Accepting sacrifice with candour of consuming fire,
Portentous through the flamelike dream of comets,
In the gentleness of candleshine like muted violins,
Or out of prisms iridescent in an orchestra of colour;
Most mysterious in the silences of pictures - Constable,
His cornfields thatched with sunlight; The Impressionists,
Whose glowing genius made the instantaneous eternal - Monet,
Painting heaven on earth; the burning forest of Van Gogh.
But today our light is frozen in a blink of cameras,
Mirrors with a memory, or disciplined in lasers.

Making light of matter, we enkindle the invisible.
The dark, atomic seeds at Nature's centre
Come to flower with ordered brilliancy;
The quick illumination of another time,
Of flashes of a future to unpeople Earth;
To carry out our thoughts across a universe,
Or put them all to sleep for ever.
Thus with every new invention we must choose -
Perfected presence's who dwell within their shining,
Or the hot, rebellious angel's hurtling downfall.

Robert Gordon

The Sea Monster Of Borve

From frothing mouth
   a turquoise tongue
      of the orange
brown, black monster
   spits at the child;

jumping the wave
   missing the beast's
      jagged jaw, child
stares at the sea
   monster of Borve.

Robert Shooter

Cheering Latin

*Siphunculated is a word rarely heard,
Almost but not quite absurd.
Ancient Latin was its source,
Later the artisan's discourse.
For if it were not for the teapot's spout,
How on earth would
The tea pour out?

*Siphunculated - having a spout.

R De B Hovell

My Obsolete Plain

As time waltzes by,
I stand.
A lost soul,
on an obsolete plain.
I watch as time falls away . . .
Seconds.
Minutes.
Hours.
Days.
All sweep past me
in a blur.
Melted together
by passing space.
A space
I'm not sure I belong in.
Am I a part of this space
or just a face,
lost in time,
sentenced to stand
on my obsolete pain?

Amanda Daniels

Golden Glory

Dawn lifted,
awakened solitaire,
tender warmth,
uncoiled sleepily.

Gradually burnished,
ferice limbs,
out stretched,
reached.

Confidently touched slowly,
recoiled suppressive,
ascend fragile withdrawal.

Darkness embraced,
chased retreated,
surrendered sun,
coiled asleep . . .

T A Peachey

The Holy Grail

It is written in one of Glastonbury's legends
That the Holy Grail to our shores,
Brought to the Tor by Joseph of Arimathea -
That revered cup of Last Supper fame.
Landing in Cornwall, Saint Joseph and his little band
Moved on to a hill called Wearyall,
Near Glastonbury, where Joseph left his hawthorn staff
In the ground - it proved a miracle.

The thorn took root, and Joseph built, of daub and wattle,
The first church on the soil of England,
Said to have existed till a Twelfth Century fire.
The Grail was buried on nearby land.
Glastonbury is named as the Isle of Avalon.
Surrounded in those days by waters,
Is it there, by barge, the dying King Arthur was borne
By three queens, from his last battleground.

King Arthur and his knights had long sought the Holy Grail.
As the Twelfth Century neared its end
The noble remains were found, in the abbey then built,
Or Arthur and his queen, Guinevere.
In summer, on flat lands of the Vale of Avalon,
A veil of mists writhes around the Tor;
Memory of the waters once covering that land,
Bearing Arthur's barge in far-off times.

Jack Finch

Ode To A Lancashire Parakeet

Sitting on the slope of a hill one day
I looked down on a moorland stream
And listened to summer.
All at once there shot up,
Across my vision,
Tropical colour -

Its coarse chatter
Reminding me of passing terraced houses
And hearing the same.
I twitched like the keenest of ornithologists
As I followed its flight.

Eventually seeing no more of it
And having rested,
I walked on home.
I forgot that tropical colour
As the year passed.

Early the following spring
On a sheep path I walked
Beside that same moorland stream.
There on the ground,
In front of me,
Lay the body of a parakeet.

The sight saddened me,
Disturbed me
And depressed me.
But it was not all me.
It was the thought.

That a parakeet bred far from its native family
Had made a flight to freedom
And seemingly had found itself a place of refuge.
It had survived the mocking of skylarks;
Even rooks and crows had failed to have its life.

Yet . . .
Here it was, dead.
The worst of the winter now over with.
If Jesus was right in what he said?
Then heaven was surely crying now.

David A Chamberlain

Nocturne

Midnight dreams, bid natures cloudless glory stay
Selenes timeless grace whispers to man bellow.
Her silence immortal and blessed in solitude
knows, best shriven by night mans tortured day.
In evening sky's darkened shadow
on chilly winds blow rude.

Ponders starry space natures frantic powers
betrays universal form, humanities mastery compares.
Tracing Earthly elements in material compositions
fragile bodies erotic dream strike only in midnight hours.
Dark beauty of natures internal workings shares,
within mans nocturnal emissions.

Beneath cherry trees coppiced boughs
where leafy arms of weeping willows caress.
In sequested lower watchman to the night
slender necks red lined discordant mew
his Siamese hunters instincts full arouse.
By midnight natures sacred forms address,
his feline shadow; puzzles mans existence, by moonlight
glittering ageless eyes reflecting ancient blue.

Masking primevil thoughts, lights slowly moving pace
the sky a silent cardboard still,
velvet calm, in shades of silken grey on broken blue.
Philosophy in man finds, ever constantly changing truth
healing our pain in purple pansies faded violet face.
Days anguished carline thistle, stabs mans saddened will
asking what in the universe is true?
Navigates, our ancestral temples, crystal mirrored proof.

In embodied spirit, humble flesh,a new dawn
from Lavenders fragmented intellect, night tells.
Remembers honeysuckles perfumed shade, of yesterday
natures borrowed wisdom's diamonds sharp Camomile lawn.
Saw wintry gales ply ornate windchimes silver bells
and their hidden thoughts,among rose and purple heather play.

Stray carillion melodies resonant chime
sweet dulcet tones performed, rejoice at midnight.
Dusky pink shadows, scent my open kitchen door
when all else in slumber steals and the moment is all mine.
Treasured joys, Arcadian pleasure, moons smoky twilight
Moons healing balm; showing man; Natures more divine law.

Mary-Jayne Evans

Guenevere

Evening's rose-silver mist,
And fragrance of a fairy tale,
Brings fairy starlight. Night descends
In folds of satin deepest-blue.

Violet wine. The hazy shine
Of spiral-twisted scarlet candles
Tulip-capped with flame.
Guenevere - swan, rose, and stars . . .
Sprays of violets lie entwined
Around her lovely name.

Darkly seen through diamond panes
Are twilight holly-bushes, steeped
In autumn's smoky cold.
Behind a vast embroidered screen,
Guenevere the lovely Queen
Devoutly reads her holy book,
Its cover stamped in gold.

Edward Francis

Cockcrow Over Bethlehem

One eye at rest, the other drinks askance
a servant girl. Remembering too much
he prays he might revisit now
the birthplace, unravelling
proud industries of time, undoing
nets beneath a keening sky, pursuing
artless threads to Bethlehem.

Time's draught now whistles mockingly
around and through the stable walls.

As evening chill frisks into life the flames of love
he hears a gentle lullaby and sees
a tiny woman with a concave breast
pour out her goodness into baby's earnest cheeks
while squeezing salt-stained smile. Sighing steam
she kisses dimpled hand and in the sooty cold
pangs out post-natal echo of a loud, eternal Yes.
Maria swallows painfully. Her purple hands
move deftly, wrapping Karim's wrinkled legs and arms
in anything she finds. Silently
she scans the clinic echo of her London squat
for Pampers, curtains, anything.
Ashni brings her rags
and fills a dirty flask
with water from the man next door.

Tomorrow we must travel. Another pilgrim day
which promises a ditch.

Prophets, we hear, fare better far from home.
Have hope, they say: will travel.
Blunt inhumanity lurks miserably
in human hearts and keeps strange company
with subjugated love. But strain to hear the stifled call
to hills and lacerating cross. And Peter,
Do not be afraid. before the child was born,
you had been forgiven seventy times seven.

Louise Swanston

Mal de Mar

fish fell in love with his wristwatch
its cod-flesh phosphorescence
tethered at the naval to an iron lung
in salt water amnion
menstruum or mulligrubs
gyres on a mandrel this ambergris
a swim's soiled togs spread wet on greet linoleum
maelstrom of migraine lunches
a cuttlefish slithers
liver slick
slice wide the bed's dark abdomen
nauseous nine green gallons
little Jonah slid out
mooncalf miscarriage
wrapped in cellophane
rönten rays bathe the egg-faced Madonna
counting fingers with her jackanapes

Nicholas Johnston

First Poem In Months

There is something about
The pen's conspiracy of silence
That draws the mind
To live in its reflection.

The page spreads - a luminous cage
Suspended eye against line
A purity that cannot break
This sense of despair in its layered shine.

I find myself picking out the antipodean shadow
Of hopes restless bones
Pitting belief against played out rotting words
For something that goes beyond diction.

But there is nothing more
Only the crude sparkle of past distances
That I have stowed
Like a sack full of rich green avocados.

G A Youldon-Hockey

The First Supper

No longer Piscean shod,
We are freed
From swimming in the waters
Of collective control.

Now, with Aquarian pitchers
On our heads
We carry
Our own water and food supply.

We are the masters of our fates
The captains of our souls.

Spiritual empowerment revisited.

Power . . . resources . . . finances . . . abilities . . .
Gifts
To share with one another
And with all
Symbolised by the sharing of our
Packed lunches
At the First Supper.

J C Crowe

The Church

I stand at the back, hesitantly
below the organ pipes.
The ceiling, blue, arches over me
like the Egyptian god of the sky.
Thoughts fill me, both pagan and
Christian; they mingle now
I have returned here.

It is dark, and the candles flicker
the smell of half dead flowers
from the gardens of the still Faithful . . .
and the incense, smell of my youth.
I remember the place of my childhood,
how big it seems, and how
it should seem smaller.
Perhaps it means more to me now.

I remember, I have been
in many churches, but here . . .
I once confessed who I was
without ever saying my name.

Marco Farina